Sail in the Boat
with
Jesus

AN ACTION RHYME BOOK

Sail in the Boat
with
Jesus

Leena Lane and Chris Saunderson

Say 'All aboard!'

All aboard!

Climb into the boat.

Climb into the boat, with Jesus.

Wave to people on the shore

Wave! Wave!
The boat's setting off.
The boat's setting off, with Jesus.

Yawn and stretch

Yawn! Yawn!
What a busy day.
What a busy day, with Jesus.

Hush! Hush!
He's fallen asleep.
Keep nice and quiet, for Jesus.

Put finger over lips

Rock! Rock!

The waves rock the boat!

The waves rock the boat, with Jesus!

Rock from side to side

Clap hands and stamp feet

Crash! Crash!
There's thunder and lightning!
There's a terrible storm, near Jesus!

Shout 'Help!'

Help! Help!
We might all drown!
The boat might sink, with Jesus!

Swim! Swim!
We might have to swim!
We might have to swim, with Jesus!

Swim with your arms

Tug your sleeve

Wake up! Wake up!
'Please save us, Lord!'
'Please save us!' they shout, to Jesus.

No, no!
'I'll keep you safe.
'Don't be afraid!' says Jesus.

Shake your head

Hold arms up high

Be still! Be still!
He's calming the storm.
The wind and sea listen to Jesus.

Thank you! Thank you!
The storm has gone quiet.
Now we're all safe, thanks to Jesus!

Clasp hands together and smile

Published in the UK by Scripture Union

207-209 Queensway, Bletchley,

Milton Keynes, Bucks MK2 2EB

ISBN 1 84427 095 5

First edition 2005

Copyright © AD Publishing Services Ltd

1 Churchgates, The Wilderness,

Berkhamsted, Herts HP4 2UB

Text copyright © 2005 AD Publishing Ltd, Leena Lane

Illustrations copyright © 2005 Chris Saunderson

Editorial Director Annette Reynolds

Art Director Gerald Rogers

Pre-production Krystyna Hewitt

Production John Laister

Printed and bound in China